PIANO · VOCAL · GUITAR

Best of
BILL
ANDERSON

T0039511

ISBN 978-1-4584-0509-8

HAL•LEONARD®
CORPORATION
7777 W. BLUEMOUND RD. P.O.BOX 13819 MILWAUKEE, WI 53213

Visit Hal Leonard Online at
www.halleonard.com

A little over fifty years ago, I moved to Nashville, Tennessee, for the sole purpose of becoming a country music songwriter.

Not a recording artist, not a featured performer on the Grand Ole Opry, and most definitely not the host of television game shows nor an actor on a daytime soap opera, all of which I ultimately became. In the beginning, I simply wanted to write songs for other people to sing. I figured if I could do that, my dreams would all come true.

Well, those dreams came true time and time again. You are holding a large portion of the proof in your hands.

People ask me all the time how many songs I have written. My answer is, "I don't know. I've been too busy writing them to stop and count." It sounds flippant, I know, but it's also the truth.

Regardless of the total, it was difficult narrowing the list down to these twenty-two. These aren't necessarily the songs that went the highest in the charts. Nor are they necessarily the most popular songs among my fans. But, as a whole, they are the most impactful songs of my career. Each one holds a special place in my life, and quite possibly in yours.

I hope you will enjoy visiting them again, whether at your piano, with your guitar, or just curled up in your favorite easy chair. All I ask is that you handle them with care.

After all, they are like my children.

Bill Anderson

CONTENTS

CITY LIGHTS

Words and Music by
BILL ANDERSON

COLD HARD FACTS OF LIFE

Words and Music by
BILL ANDERSON

GIVE IT AWAY

Words and Music by JAMEY JOHNSON,
BILL ANDERSON and BUDDY CANNON

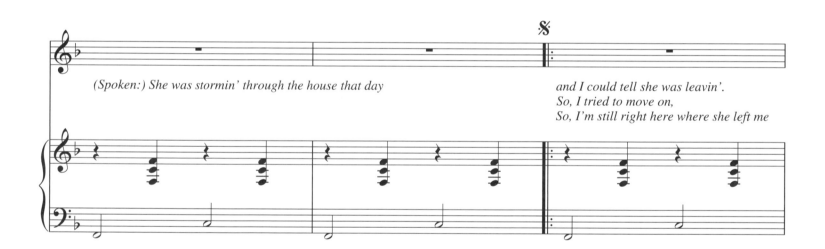

(Spoken:) She was stormin' through the house that day

and I could tell she was leavin'.
So, I tried to move on,
So, I'm still right here where she left me

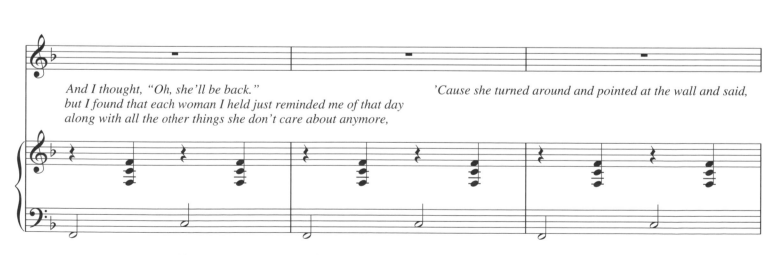

And I thought, "Oh, she'll be back."
but I found that each woman I held just reminded me of that day
along with all the other things she don't care about anymore,

'Cause she turned around and pointed at the wall and said,

D.S. al Coda

CODA F

I've got a fur - nished house, ___ a

dia - mond ring ___ and a lone - ly bro - ken heart ___ full of love ___

Bb N.C. F7

___ and I can't e - ven give it a - way.

I GET THE FEVER

Words and Music by
BILL ANDERSON

I get _____ the fe - ver _____ to _____
I get _____ the fe - ver _____ to _____

pack up _____ and leave _____ here _____ and _____
pack up _____ and leave _____ here, _____ and _____

wan - der wild _____ like the wind.
I think may - be I'll do just that to - mor - row.

This town's _ too full _____ of _____
This town's _ too full _____ of _____

mem - 'ries of cruel _____ love, ___ and I can't stand ___ it
mem - 'ries of cruel _____ love. ___ Ev - 'ry - where ___ I turn,

see - in' her _____ with him.⎫
there's pain _____ and sor - row.⎭
Ev - er - y time ___

___ I hear ___ a bud - dy say, ___ "He's put lots of dust ___

___ and clay ___ be - tween him and yes - ter - day," _____

I MAY NEVER GET TO HEAVEN

Words and Music by BUDDY KILLEN
and BILL ANDERSON

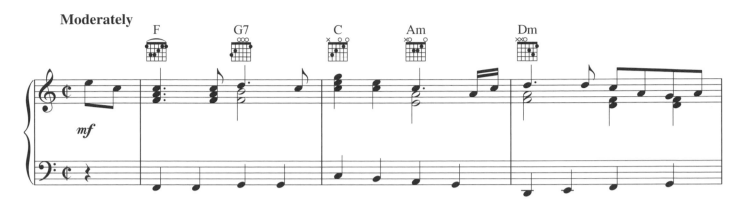

I walked with you and talked with you and

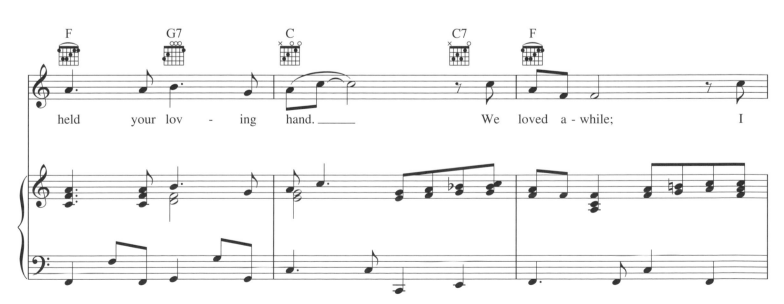

held your lov - ing hand. _____ We loved a - while; I

THE LORD KNOWS I'M DRINKING

Words and Music by
BILL ANDERSON

Recorded a half step lower.

ONCE A DAY

Words and Music by
BILL ANDERSON

Moderately fast

When you found ____ some-bod-y new, ____ I thought I
I'm so glad ____ that I'm not like ____ a girl I

nev-er would ____ knew one time. ____

for-get ____ you for
She lost ____ the one for she

I thought then ____ I nev-er could. ____
loved and slow-ly lost ____ her mind.

But time ____
She ____

Recorded a half step lower.

A LOT OF THINGS DIFFERENT

Words and Music by DEAN DILLON
and BILL ANDERSON

MAMA SANG A SONG

Words and Music by
BILL ANDERSON

Gently

God put a song in the heart of an an-gel and

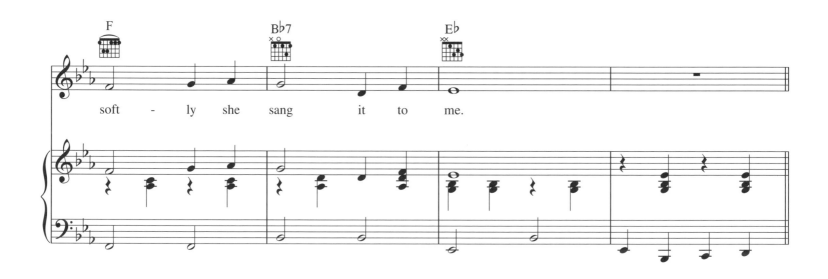

soft - ly she sang it to me.

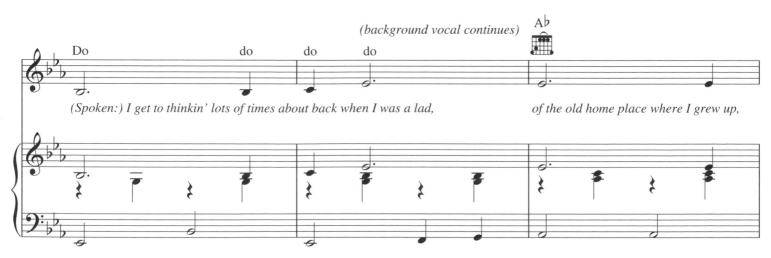

Do   do do do

(background vocal continues)

(Spoken:) I get to thinkin' lots of times about back when I was a lad,   of the old home place where I grew up,

of the days, both good and bad.   *My overalls were hand-me-downs.*

My shoes were full of holes.   *I used to walk four miles to school every day,*   *through the rain, the sleet and the cold.*

I've seen the nights when my daddy would cry for the things that his family would need.

But all he ever got was a badland farm and seven hungry mouths to feed.

And he'd read it, read it loud and long. And I always felt that maybe our home was blessed when Daddy would say,

"Mama, sing a song." Sister left home first, I guess. And then Bob, and then Tommy, and then Dan.

By then, Dad's hair was turning white, and I had to be my mama's little man. But it seemed that as my

daddy's back grew weak, my mother's faith just grew strong.

And those were the greatest days of all: when Mama sang a song. Rock of Ag - es,

cleft for me, let me hide

my - self in Thee. Do do *(background vocal continues)* *I guess the house is still standing,*

I don't get to go back much anymore. *No voice is left to fill those halls and no steps*

PO' FOLKS

Words and Music by
BILL ANDERSON

D.S. al Coda

We was po' —

CODA

ta - ble with love — 'cause that's what you do when you're

po' folks and we was-n't noth - in' but po' — folks. My

Repeat and Fade | **Optional Ending**

mom and my dad — was po' folks. My po' folks.
broth - er and my sis - ter was po' folks. My
dog and my cat — was po' folks. *ad lib.*

SAGINAW, MICHIGAN

Words and Music by DON WAYNE
and BILL ANDERSON

I was born in Sag-i-naw, Mich-i-gan.
I loved a girl in Sag-i-naw, Mich-i-gan,
I wrote my love in Sag-i-naw, Mich-i-gan.
Her dad met me in Sag-i-naw, Mich-i-gan.

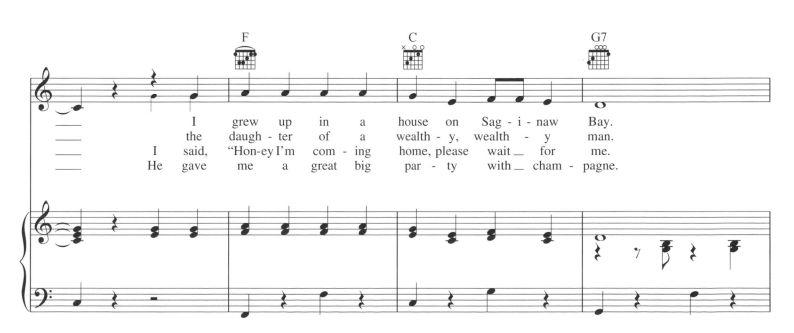

I grew up in a house on Sag-i-naw Bay.
the daugh-ter of a wealth-y, wealth-y man.
I said, "Hon-ey I'm com-ing home, please wait for me.
He gave me a great big par-ty with cham-pagne.

My dad was a poor,   hard - work - ing Sag - i - naw fish - er - man.
But he called me   that son of a Sag - i - naw fish - er - man,
You can tell your _ dad   I'm com - ing back a rich - er man.
Then he said, _ "Son,   you're a wise young am - bi - tious man.

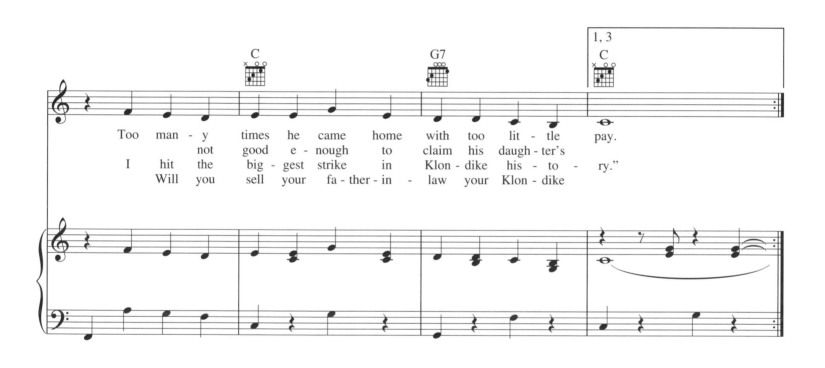

Too man - y times he came home with too lit - tle pay.
not good e - nough to claim his daugh - ter's
I hit the big - gest strike in Klon - dike his - to - ry."
Will you sell your fa - ther - in - law your Klon - dike

1, 3
C

2, 4
C

hand.   Now I'm up here in A - las - ka
claim?"   Now he's up there in A - las - ka

SLIPPIN' AWAY

Words and Music by
BILL ANDERSON

THE TIP OF MY FINGERS

Words and Music by
BILL ANDERSON

SOMETIMES

Words and Music by
BILL ANDERSON

STILL

Words and Music by
BILL ANDERSON

(Spoken:) I've lost count of the hours and I've lost track of the days.

In fact, I've lost just about everything since you went away, everything, that is, except the memories you left me.
(Sung:) (I   love   you   still.) _____

And that's one thing that no one can mar. I don't know who you're with, I don't even know where you've gone. My only hope is that

someday you might hear this song and you'll know that I wrote it especially for you and I love you, wherever you are.
(I   love   you ___   still.) _____

Still, af-ter all this time, __ still, you're still on my mind. __

I love you __ still. _____

(Spoken:) *This flame in my heart is like an eternal fire, for every day*

it burns hotter and every day it burns higher and I haven't been able to put out one little flicker, not even with all of these tears.
(Sung:) (I love you still.) _____

TOO COUNTRY

Words and Music by BILL ANDERSON
and CHUCK CANNON

TWO TEARDROPS

Words and Music by BILL ANDERSON
and STEVE WARINER

(Two tear-drops.)
(Two tear-

drops.)
Two tear-drops were float- in' down the riv-er. One tear-drop said

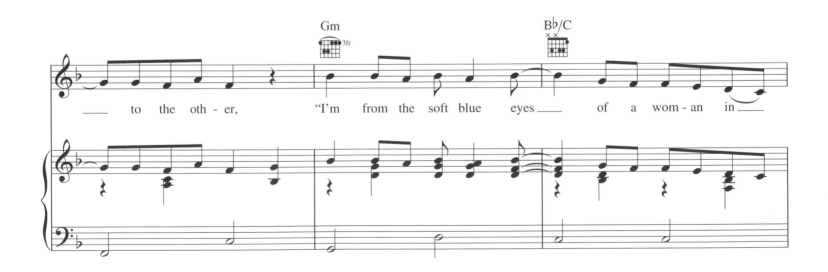

to the oth- er, "I'm from the soft blue eyes of a wom-an in

WHICH BRIDGE TO CROSS
(Which Bridge to Burn)

Words and Music by BILL ANDERSON
and VINCE GILL

cross - roads _____ with just one con - cern: _____ Which bridge _____ to

cross _____ and which bridge to burn. _____ I

WHEN TWO WORLDS COLLIDE

Words and Music by ROGER MILLER
and BILL ANDERSON

Moderate Waltz

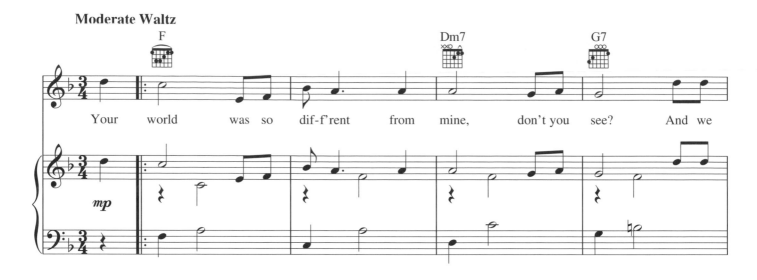

Your world was so dif-f'rent from mine, don't you see? And we

could-n't be close though we tried. _____ We both reached for

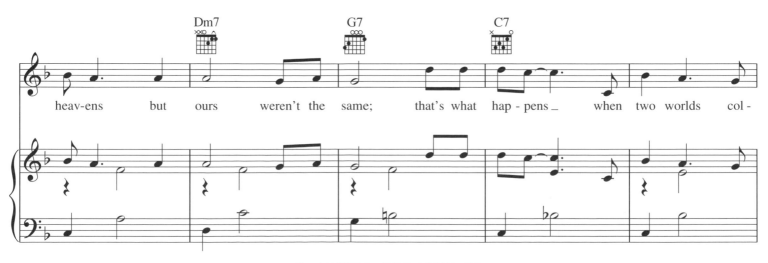

heav-ens but ours weren't the same; that's what hap-pens ___ when two worlds col-

WHISKEY LULLABY

Words and Music by BILL ANDERSON
and JON RANDALL

WILD WEEK END

Words and Music by
BILL ANDERSON

* Recorded a half step lower.

WISH YOU WERE HERE

Words and Music by BILL ANDERSON,
DONALD EWING and DEBBIE MOORE

Moderately

They kissed good-bye _____ at the ter - mi - nal gate.

She said, "You're gon-na be late _____ if you don't go." _____

She got a call____ that night,____ but it was-n't from him.

It did-n't sink in____ right a-way.____